How We See Things

John Stringer

The Sun is the brightest light source we see. Never look straight at the Sun. Looking directly at it – even for a moment – can permanently damage your eyes.

But we need light to see. Without a light source, we can't see anything.

Sunlight is **reflected** from clouds, and the surfaces all around us. So sunlight fills our daytime lives from every direction. The back of the house may be shady, but the rooms are not totally dark because the Sun's light is reflected into them. We live our lives in a sea of sunlight.

We are rarely in total darkness. You think your bedroom is dark at night, yet there is still some light. It might be light reflected from the Moon, or light from a source somewhere in the house.

There is complete darkness in a deep cave. There is no light at all. You need a torch to see anything. When you switch on the torch, you can see the objects you shine the torch at. This cave has light shining in from a hole in the roof.

How we see was a mystery for many thousands of years. Two thousand years ago, scientists like Ptolemy and Euclid believed that we saw because our eyes sent out magic rays. These rays touched an object, and so we saw it. But they couldn't explain why these rays did not work in the dark.

Abu Hasan Ibn al-Haitham or Alhazen was born over 1000 years ago in Iraq. He was one of the Islamic scientists whose ideas changed science. Alhazen used observation, ideas and investigation. He wrote over two hundred books. European scientists like Roger Bacon and Leonardo da Vinci read them.

Alhazen explored the way we see. He observed how light was bent as it passed through water. He used these ideas to investigate the way that lenses **magnify**. He observed the way that the Sun appeared to change colour as it set at the end of the day.

Alhazen did not believe in magic rays. He imagined that the eye was a receiver of light. So he thought that when he looked at a candle, the light from the flame entered his eye and he could see it. A candleholder is not a source of light.

Perhaps light from the candle flame could be reflected from it. Then when the reflected light entered his eye, he saw the candleholder with that reflected light.

If he blew the candle out, he could no longer see the flame. But he couldn't see the candleholder, either. He needed the light from the candle flame.

Alhazen tried some investigations with light. He worked inside a dark room with a hole in the wall. Outside, he hung lanterns. He found that he could only see things in the room when the lantern light shone on them.

This is because your eye is a light collector. The front of your eye focuses the light on the back of your eye. The part of your eye that is **sensitive** to light is called the retina. Light falls on your retina. Your retina sends signals to your brain.

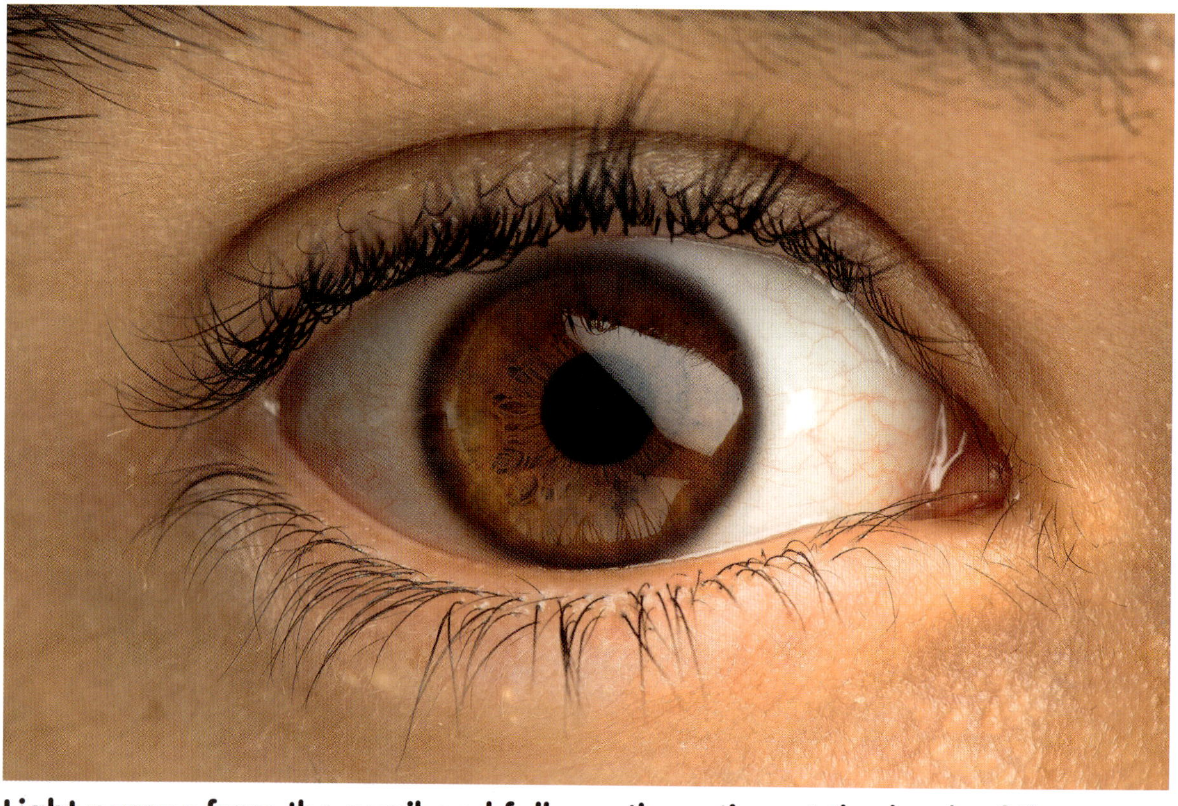

Light passes from the pupil and falls on the retina at the back of the eye.

We need a light source to see in the dark. We see because light is reflected from everything. It is reflected best from **mirrors** and shiny surfaces, and from white surfaces, too. It is not reflected well from black and dark surfaces. Road signs and reflective clothing reflect most of the light falling on them. They appear to shine with their own light.

But they don't. Like the eyes of a cat, they reflect back the light shining on them. **Nocturnal** creatures like cats need to make the best use of low light. Their eyes are lined with a reflective surface. Light falling on their eyes goes through the retina twice. It is this **reflection** that makes their eyes 'glow in the dark'.

Every surface reflects light. Even transparent surfaces reflect some light, though most of the light passes through. Shiny surfaces reflect more light than duller ones, and really smooth surfaces can reflect light as it strikes them. They act as a mirror and reflect an image. The angle at which a light beam hits a reflective surface and the angle at which it reflects off are the same.

We see objects because light from a light source is reflected into our eyes. We see because light passes through transparent materials and less well through translucent ones. We can see images reflected in mirrors.

Because light is reflected directly back at us by a mirror, we see the world reversed. Our left pocket is reflected back to our left, so appears to be on the right when we look at the image. This boy's tie is pulled to the right, but in the mirror it appears to be pulled to the left.

Smooth and creased kitchen foil both reflect the same amount of light. But the creased foil reflects differently from the smooth.

When foil is smooth, it reflects the light from your face straight back at you so you can see your reflection. When it is slightly creased, some of the light reflects back to you. But some light is reflected off in other directions because the light hits different parts of the paper at different angles.

When the foil is heavily creased, the light is spread over a wide area in lots of directions and there is no clear reflected image.
But the same amount of light is still reflected.

White light is a mixture of colours of light. Objects look coloured because they reflect or absorb (take in) the different colours in white light. A golf ball is white because it reflects all the light that falls on it. Its refection is white. A lemon absorbs all the **wavelengths** of light except yellow. It reflects the yellow light into our eyes.

A black bag absorbs all the wavelengths of light and reflects almost none, so it looks black to us.

Convex

Concave

Curved mirrors change the direction of light. Concave mirrors make the light beams converge. They can be focused on one point. Convex mirrors make the light beams diverge. They are spread widely.

Security mirrors are convex mirrors, collecting light from all around a shop so that all the shop can be seen.

Shaving and makeup mirrors are concave. They magnify your image. Fairground mirrors are both concave and convex. They distort your image.

When light passes through materials like glass, water or plastic, it slows down. As light enters and leaves a glass lens, it changes speed and direction. This is called **refraction**.

The Roman Emperor Nero made use of refraction to view performances in the Roman Arena through a **fragment** of emerald. The light was bent by the emerald. It was just the right shape to aid his failing eyesight.

If you put a pencil or a straw in water, its image is bent when the light passes through the water.

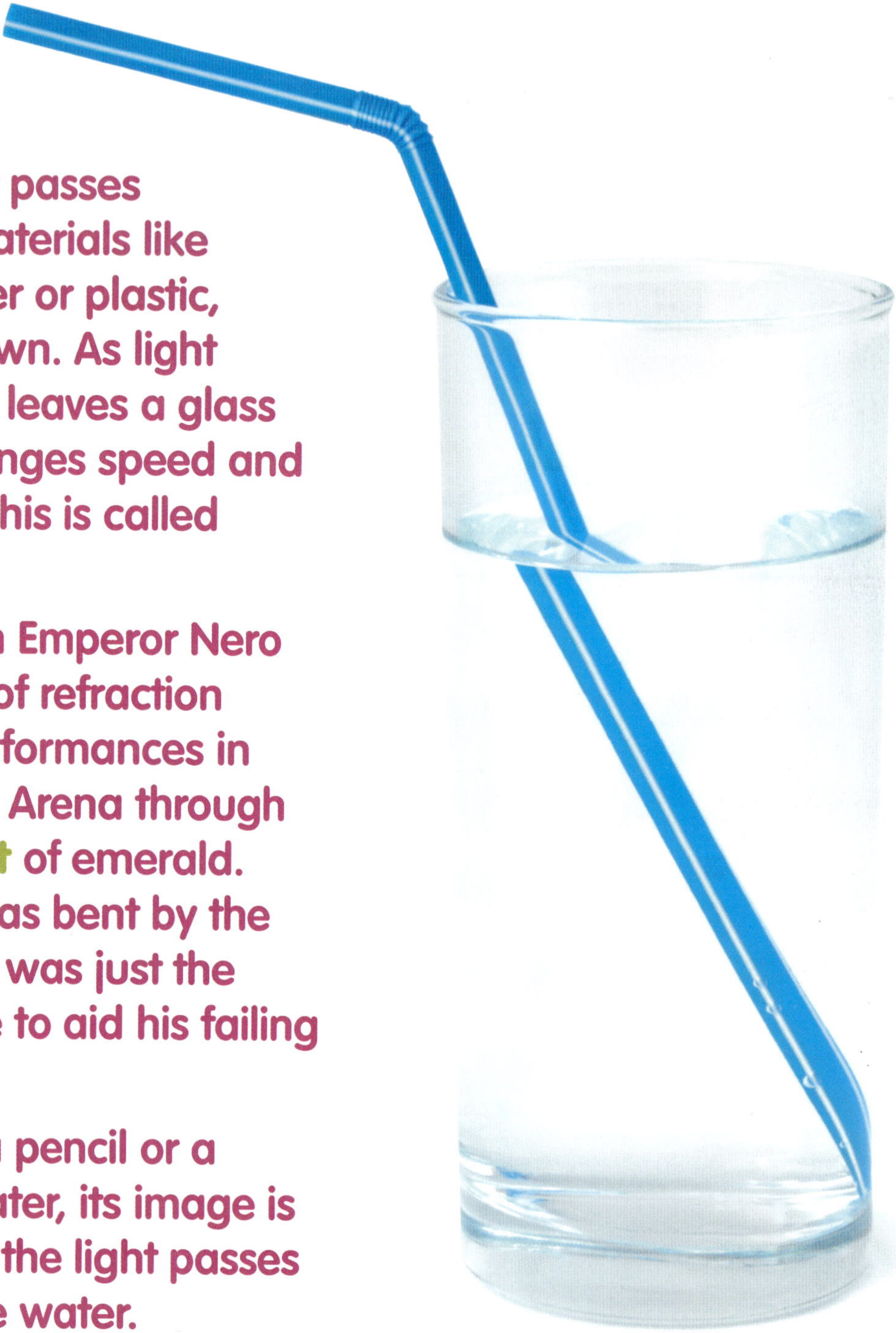

Light changes direction when it travels from one material to another. This is because light travels at different speeds in different materials. The side of the light wave that first enters the new material slows down before the other side of the light wave. This causes the light to bend.

Glass and water both slow down and bend light. The different colours that make up white light travel at different speeds through glass and water, so the faster moving colours bend less than the slower moving colours.

This splits the light into different colours. We call this band of colours a spectrum, or a rainbow.

Rainbows appear in **moist** air. To see a rainbow, you need to be between the rain and the Sun. Then every raindrop bends the light and reflects it back to the Sun. Each drop reflects only one colour. Many raindrops form its spectrum of light.

A morning rainbow forms in the West. This is the direction that storms generally come from. It is a sign of bad weather coming. Evening rainbows appear in the East. They tell you that the stormy weather has passed.

Isaac Newton made a spectrum using a triangular block of glass – a prism. He worked in a dark room. He made a small hole in the window blind. A ray of light came through. He passed the ray through a triangular block of glass. The white light was split into colours.

Isaac Newton saw six spectrum colours: red, orange, yellow, green, blue and violet. He added a seventh colour, indigo, to his spectrum of six because seven was a magical number!

But Isaac Newton had noticed that the light through that hole in the shutter, 'about one third part of an inch broad', came in as a circle; but it left the prism as a multi-coloured strip. So, he concluded, the light is not 'changed' – it is split. His investigation proved that the spectrum was created from the colours in white light.

He shone the colours through another prism and got the white light back.

Inside the eye, light passes through a lens, which makes a picture or image on the back of the eye. The back of the eye is called the retina and is covered with special nerve cells. These special cells react to the light and send a message to your brain to say that you are seeing something.

There is a place on the retina where the cells are packed together. This is where you see best. That's why you will turn your head or move your eye to look at something closely.

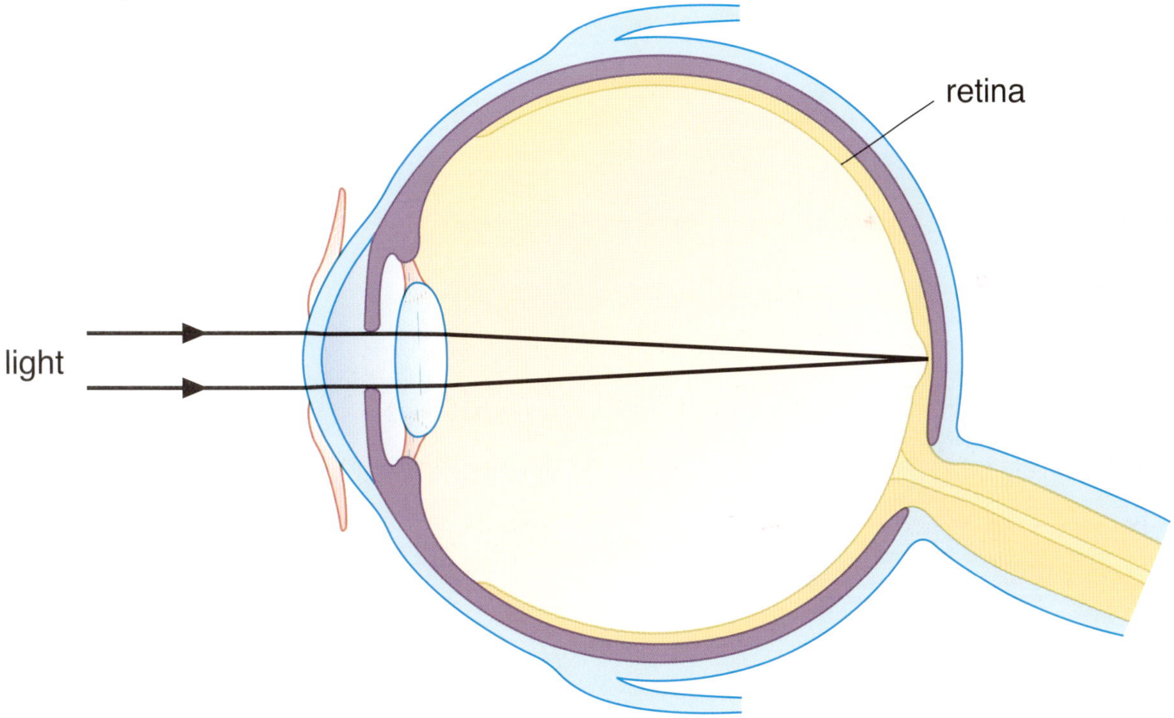

Light enters your eye through a tough cornea or window. The muscular iris can open and close to let in light. Then the lens focuses the light on the sensitive retina. Muscles can change the shape of the lens when you look close up or far away.

The retina has two kinds of light receivers: rods and cones. These send messages to the brain. The brain works out what the eye is seeing. It produces a picture you can understand. It even fills in a hole in the picture where there are no sensitive cells.

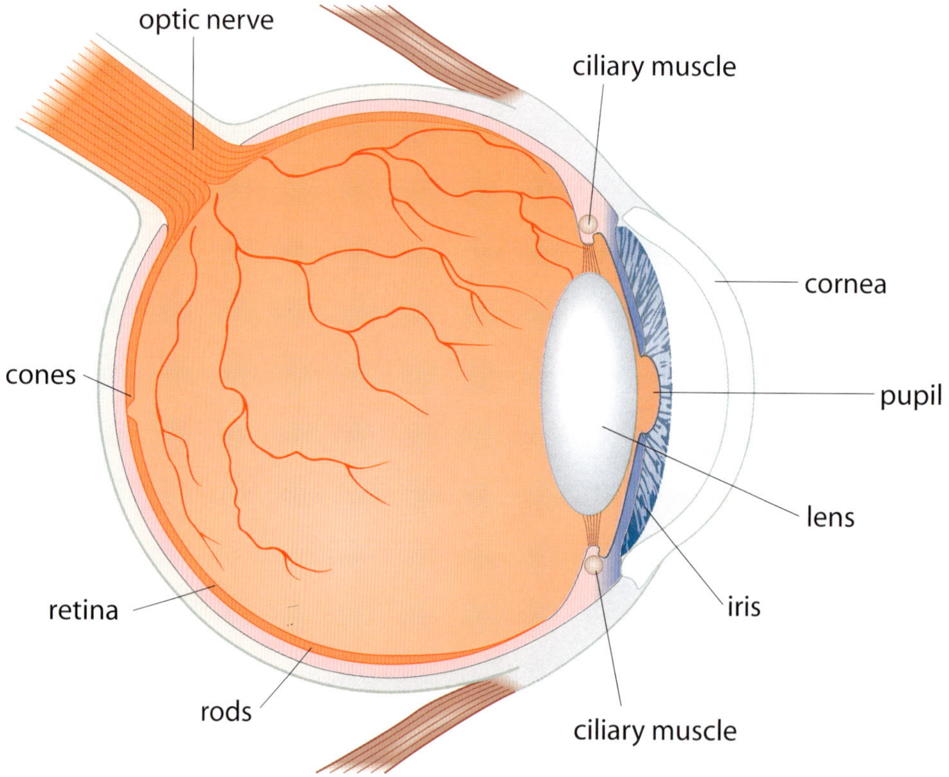

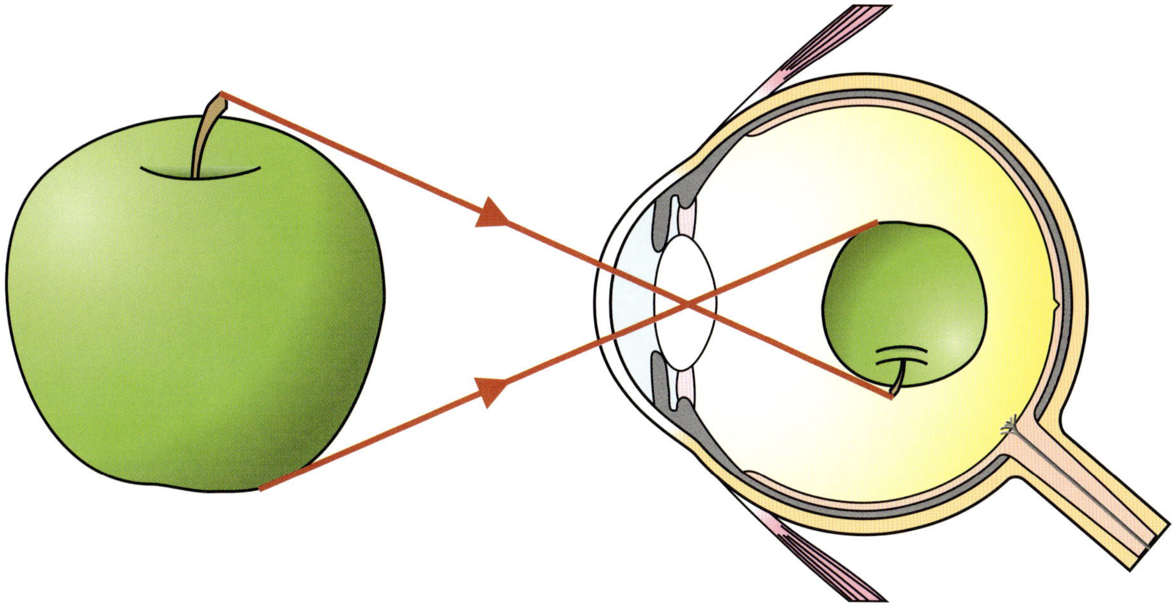

The picture that forms on the back of your eye is actually upside-down. Your brain quickly learns to turn the picture the right way up when you are a baby. Until they have picked up this trick, babies may try to grab for things hanging above their cot and miss.

A scientist tried wearing glasses that **inverted** his view, and eventually his brain got used to the idea of everything being the wrong way up. His brain made the necessary **adaptation**, and he was able to see things correctly again.

Then he took the glasses off...

A lens is a piece of plastic or glass that can make things seem to change size. Lenses work by bending light rays so they appear to come from a slightly different place. Some lenses make things look closer and bigger, while others make things look smaller and farther away.

The two main types of lens are called concave and convex. A concave lens is thin in the middle and thick at the edges and it makes light rays bend outwards or diverge. A convex lens works in the opposite way. It is thicker in the middle and thinner at the edges and light rays passing through a convex lens converge. They come together.

Short-sighted people wear glasses with concave lenses. Together with the lens of the eye, these focus a clear image in the proper place on the retina.

Long-sighted people wear convex lenses, which bend the light rays inwards to strike the eye lens at the right angle for an image to be focused on the retina.

An optical instrument makes use of one or more lenses or mirrors, or a combination of these. They change the path of light rays and produce an image. Magnifying glasses, microscopes and telescopes give a clear magnified image of things that are very small and very distant.

There are six million cones in each eye. These are special receptors for blue, green and red light, and allow us to see in colour. They work best in bright light. When the light levels are low, the rods take over. Rods can work in dim light, detecting movement and shape. You see in your dim bedroom with 120 million rods.

Some people – especially men – are born 'colour-blind'. They find it difficult to separate some colours, often red and green. This makes them much more sensitive to small colour differences and to movement. Colour-blind men made good hunters for finding deer and other camouflaged animals in woodland.

A person who is colour-blind may not see the number 15 in this circle.

Today, many people rely on spectacles to see. Robert Grosseteste first noticed that fragments of glass could make grains of sand appear larger 1000 years ago. His discovery led to the first lens. About 200 years later, an Italian monk put two lenses in a frame to make the first spectacles.

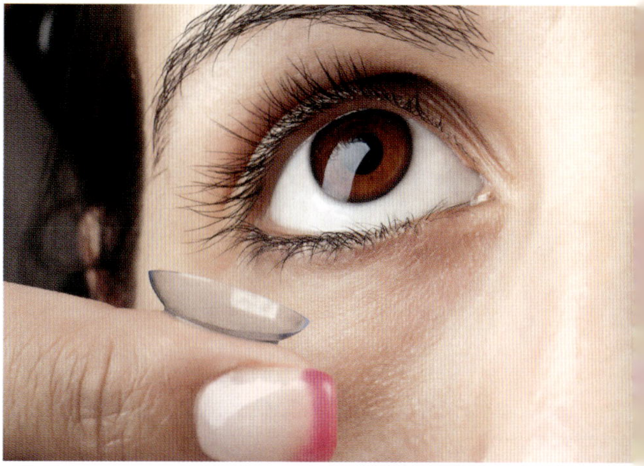

Over 100 years ago, Louis Girard of Houston invented the first **contact lens**, which covered the whole eye. One day, he broke one – the broken one covering only the cornea worked just as well!

Activity

Make a word search

Choose ten words from this book, with no more than ten letters in each word. Draw a square with ten columns and ten rows and make a word search for your friends with your ten words. The first two could be: CONVERGE and NOCTURNAL.

When you have put in your words, fill in the other squares with random letters.

C									
O									
N	O	C	T	U	R	N	A	L	
V									
E									
R									
G									
E									

Glossary

adaptation: the process of changing something to make it suitable for a new situation
concave: a concave surface is curved inwards in the middle
contact lens: a small round piece of plastic that you put on your eye to help you see clearly
converge: come together
convex: curved outwards like the surface of an eye
creased: folded or crushed so that lines appear on the material
detecting: to notice or discover something, especially something that is not easy to see or hear
diverge: spread apart
fragment: a small piece of something that has broken off or that comes from something larger
image: a reflected picture
inverted: something that's in the opposite position to the one it was in before
magnify: make something bigger
mirror: a polished surface that reflects an image
moist: slightly wet
nocturnal: active at night
receptors: nerve endings that receive information about changes in light
reflect: if a surface reflects light, heat or sound, it sends back the light (and so on) that reaches it
reflection: the action or process of light, heat or sound being thrown back from a surface
refraction: the bending of light when it travels from one material to another
reversed: the opposite way around
sensitive: easily affected or damaged by something such as a substance or temperature
translucent: allows some light to pass through and is not opaque or transparent
transparent: clear; can be easily seen through
wavelengths: the distance between two points on energy waves such as sound or light